RAISING A BRILLIANT KIDS

Parenting is considered one of the most difficult jobs in the world.

Ralph B. Davis

- Ways to discipline your child

- Listening to your Kids

- Supporting your peaceful marriage

- Saying the nice words with your kids

- Listening to help and make peace

- Know when your child is in need of something

Chapter 1 :**Learn to discipline your child**

Discipline Your Child's Behavior, Not Their Emotions
Rather than trying to force our children to not feel certain emotions (especially the ones that are inconvenient for us), we can teach them how to deal with emotions. Here are four ways to do this.
I sat on a park bench and saw it unfold.

The mom said it was time to leave and the young girl had differing plans. She wanted to stay.

This escalated into the mother's anger and the girl's tears.

Who was right?

As a teen at the time, I had opinions based on being a fifteen-year-old with wants and desires of her own. Whose wants and desires were sometimes met with, "No."

My brain connected more closely with the toddler than the mom, ironically. Both of us moved from our emotions, and our logic often showed up late in the game.

So, my initial vote went to the girl. Of course, she wanted to stay! The sun was out, the breeze was light, and there were slides, climbing frames, and friends.

But then again, maybe it was the mom who was right. She probably had errands to run and dinner to cook. Moms have a way of seeing the bigger picture like that.

I sat there playing out this scenario from both views long after they had actually left. The only conclusion I had come up with is that I was glad I didn't have to deal with that tricky parenting stuff. I was never having kids.

Becoming A Mother
That was until I did.

Jump to the present day and here I am the mom at the park telling her son it's time to leave. As my frustration escalated to anger, and my son's determination became tears of defeat, I happened to look over at an empty park bench. I remembered being the girl who watched a similar shakedown years ago. It stopped me in my tracks.

Who was right?

Neither of us.

Both of us.

My yelling and sharp tone weren't my best version, and his hitting and throwing a rock at me was not his.

Was I a bad mom? Was he a bad kid?

No, and here's why.

Becoming Aware
There is a difference between what our children do and how they feel just as there is space between how we behave and our emotions, too.

Frustration was the feeling at the park. My yelling and my son's hitting were the behaviors.

The feeling isn't wrong, bad, or broken. We were both valid in what we felt.

I wanted to leave because I had an agenda of getting dinner on the table, baths, and snuggles in before bed. He wanted to stay because the park is a fun place to be.

What is clear through our behaviors is that neither of us knew what to do with those feelings.

Emotions Tell A Story

Sometimes we tend to shut down feelings, especially if we grew up in a home where expressing emotions wasn't a safe thing to do. We tend to think that in order to teach the lesson or set the boundary, we must squash the feeling beneath it.

What I have learned is that our feelings have a purpose. They are data. For example, most times when I feel frustrated, it is because 1) I have either set an expectation in my mind and whatever is unfolding isn't meeting that expectation or 2) I am more invested in an outcome than my child. Most times when I feel resentful, it is because I have not set a firm enough emotional or physical boundary around something. I could go on, but you get the point.

Same thing for our children. Their emotions tell a story, too.

They are hungry, off-routine, tired, or have some other unmet need. They have some lagging skills like poor impulse control or emotional regulation. They want something and someone stands in their way (as in wanting to stay at the park and being told it was in fact time to leave). Thwarted desire is one of the hardest human experiences so it makes sense our children struggle with it.

If our emotions are so dang useful, then we don't want to deny or suppress them. We also can't be passive parents. So how do we set boundaries and teach lessons to raise kind, well-meaning humans without dampening their emotional experience and gaslighting our own?

Emotions Flow, Some Behaviors Are A No
The answer is discipline. Discipline means "to teach."

Emotions flow, some behaviors are a no.

So for that park scenario, it may have looked like this: I see you crying. You really want to stay at the park, don't you? It is so hard to leave.

You may insert a silly game to leave such as saying bye-bye to slide and swing as you walk to the car, or maybe you race to the tree towards the exit or play Eye Spy as you go. Or maybe you announce the transition by saying, "Do your one last thing and then it is time to head home."

And what happens if your child still doesn't want to go? Then you set an empathetic boundary. I see you want to stay. I know this feels hard. It is time to go. Would you like to hold my hand or for me to hold you on our walk to the car?

4 Ways To Teach About Emotions
Rather than trying to force our children to not feel certain emotions (especially the ones that are inconvenient for us), we can teach them how to deal with emotions. Here are four ways to do this.

1. Take a Time-In

With the help of feeling posters from the Time-In ToolKit, we adults learn how to notice, label, and channel our emotions, especially the unpleasant ones. As we learn these skills, we can share them with our children. In creating quick, simple, and daily rituals in the Time-In space, we reinforce the circuits between our feelings and regulating them. In other words, from feelings to behaviors. One of my favorite rituals is our bedtime routine in which we all snuggle in our space and revisit, "When did I feel happy, sad, calm, and mad today?"

2. Snuggle a plush

SnuggleBuddies plush toys are a playful way for children to notice how they feel inside the moment and share it with another, even when verbal communication feels tricky (or isn't developmentally available to them). In addition, the sensory input kids receive from hugging, touching, and exploring the emojis highlights and coordinates different parts of the brain.

Chapter 2:**Listening to your Kids**

Being a good listener is critical to your child's success at school. If he can't follow directions, either on the playground or in the classroom, he'll have a tough time learning. Children who are good listeners also have an advantage socially – they tend to be very good friends to others.

Here are seven ways you can help your child become a better listener:

Advertisement | page continues below
Be a good listener
Don't interrupt your child when he's telling you a story. Give him your undivided attention when he's talking – don't read the paper or carry on a conversation with someone else at the same time. Turn your attention to him when he wants to tell or show you something.

If you want him to listen to you, he needs to see that you will listen to him too. Children return the respect they receive, and children who are listened to often become good listeners themselves.

Also, listen to the way you speak. You may not be aware of it, but your communication style may sound a lot like the one your parents used. Pay attention to what you say – and how you say it – to see if there are some habits you'd like to change.

Give clear, simple directions for everyday tasks
Get in the habit of giving your child simple instructions. Make eye contact with her, and say, "Please go into the bathroom and wash your hands. Then get your backpack and meet me downstairs."

Keep in mind what's age appropriate. A 2-year-old can probably only handle a two-step instruction like, "Get your backpack and meet me downstairs." A 3- or 4-year-old may be able to handle a little more.

As she becomes a better listener, you can add another task or two. In this way, you're not only teaching your child to listen well, but also to be independent.

Praise good listening
Saying "thanks for being such a good listener" reinforces your child's desire to listen. Make a special point of praising him when he follows directions the first time.

If you tell your child "you can have two more cookies," then give her two cookies – not three or four. Otherwise your child will only tune you out once she figures out that you don't stick to your word.

Be consistent with consequences
If you tell your child that you will leave the park if he continues to stand up in the swing, follow through

without giving him another chance. Your child will be more inclined to do what he's asked when he understands that his actions have clear, enforceable consequences.

Read aloud together
The time you spend reading together prepares your child for story time at school. She'll be expected to sit still for longer and longer periods of time, so help her practice listening at home. Ask her to tell you what happened in the story as you read.

But don't force your fidgety preschooler to listen to books she's not interested in – this will make her less, not more, interested in reading. For younger preschoolers, stick to activity books that let her touch, point, or name objects.

Chapter 3:**Supporting your peaceful marriage**

Together with their family and friends, each couple is full of hopes and dreams for their future life together. But the road to a happy marriage is far from easy. And as today's divorce statistics demonstrate all too well, many couples opt not to complete the journey.

It would be easy to blame our high rate of marital failure on things like not spending enough quality time together, allowing bitterness and resentment to build in our hearts and failing to keep communication lines open. There's no end to books, articles and seminars that tell you how to improve these and many other aspects of your relationship. But while quality time, forgiveness and communication are vitally important to creating a happy marriage, if such things aren't happening, it's usually a sign of a much deeper problem. And until this problem is addressed, no amount of external behavior modification will work.

To get a hint of what this deeper issue might be, let's take a look at the following Scripture passage:

One of them, an expert in the law, tested him [Jesus] with this question: "Teacher, which is the greatest commandment in the
"'Love the Lord your God with all your heart and with all your soul and with all your mind.'

This is the first and greatest commandment. And the second is like it:

'Love your neighbor as yourself.' All the Law and the Prophets hang on these two commandments.

I believe that virtually every marital problem can be traced back to one or both partners failing to abide by these two laws. The same is true of any relationship. The minute we begin to focus on our own wants and needs over those of God or our partner; we're destined for trouble.

Experiencing communication problems in your marriage? How often do you really focus on listening to what your partner (or God) has to say instead of insisting on more airtime? Feeling bitterness and resentment growing toward your partner? When was the last time you brought him or her before the Lord in prayer and truly thanked God for your relationship? Struggling to find quality time together? How about praying with your partner and asking God how he would like you to use your time?

As you begin to do these things, you'll notice that your focus automatically starts to shift away from you and your desires and over to God and your partner. As a result, communication problems begin to improve, anger and resentment fade away and you naturally want to spend more time together. Of course, you can't expect such changes to happen overnight. Your relationship is also bound to face financial pressures, child-rearing issues and other problems that are beyond your control. But if you commit your relationship to God and make a conscious decision each day to put God and your partner first, your marriage will be able to weather any storm. Not only that; you'll also have plenty of fun together along the way!

Have you struggled to find happiness in your marriage? Perhaps it's time you and your spouse invited God to direct your relationship. If you would like to do so, we encourage you to pray the following:

With this book, you'll find powerful mindfulness skills for calming your own stress response when difficult emotions arise. You'll also discover strategies for cultivating respectful communication, effective conflict resolution, and reflective listening. In the process, you'll learn to examine your own unhelpful patterns and ingrained reactions that reflect the generational habits shaped by your parents, so you can break the cycle and respond to your children in more skillful ways.

When children experience a parent reacting with kindness and patience, they learn to act with kindness as well—thereby altering generational patterns for a kinder, more compassionate future. With this essential guide, you'll see how changing your own "autopilot reactions" can create a lasting positive impact, not just for your kids, but for generations to

Chapter **4: Saying positive things to your Kids**

Positive Things to Say to Your Child
66 Positive Things You Should Be Saying to Your Child

Being a channel of positivity — true positivity, not the toxic kind — takes tremendous strength. After all, looking on the negative side can be a form of self-protection — if you anticipate the bad stuff, maybe you won't be as hurt when it happens. Being kind, loving, and hopeful can feel scary, like you're opening yourself up to being hurt. But as anyone who's found the strength to lead with positivity can tell you, when we're able to do so, it pays dividends. Our words, actions, and attitude have ripple effects, and our positive behavior has the potential to impact who knows how many people throughout the day. And that's a lesson worth demonstrating to our children. It's especially important to re-emphasize the power of positivity to our kids as we ease out of the pandemic. It has been an overwhelming past couple of years, more so for a young child, so establishing warmth and positivity within your household is crucial. And one fantastic way to do this is through positive affirmations for kids. While it may seem like a small gesture, encouraging words can have a truly lasting effect on your little ones. Kids are like sponges, and you never know which phrase they'll latch on to, and remember for years after you say it, becoming something they repeat to themselves to help get them through tough times, or maybe becoming something they pass on to friends, wanting to spread the joy. Here are 66 positive and encouraging things to say to your child on a daily basis, toImage make sure they know you're always in their corner.

Being a parent is the most difficult aspect of being a human. It is special in that it requires little to no training, has a lot of room for improvement, leads to continued failure, and requires long, tough hours

In order to break out from reactive parenting or the need for greater parenting knowledge to provide your children with a better upbringing, Raising Good Humans offers useful and doable solutions. A peaceful society begins with kind, self-assured, and compassionate children. To have a strong influence on this as an adult will require your success in raising your children's trust and showing respectful parenting.

It's difficult work being a parent! And many parents respond in stressful situations unthinkingly, often by shouting while not realizing the harm it would do to their children. Sometimes you can be so stress to maintain control, and go from one spot to another on time and in tact rather than constantly responding automatically. This book provides more information on how to handle your kid in a stressful form.

Positive Things to Say to Your Child

I'm grateful for you.
You make me proud.
Your words are meaningful.
You have great ideas.
I love being your parent.
You don't have to be perfect to be great.
Your opinions matter.
You are important.
You are loved.
I believe you.
I believe in you.
This family wouldn't be the same without you.
You are valuable.
You can say no.
You can say yes.
I know you did your best.
You were right.
I accept who you are.
We can try your way.
You are helpful.
You are worth it.
You make me happy.
I love your creativity.
Being around you is fun.
I can't wait to hear about it.
Don't be afraid to be you.
You're making a difference.
I'm excited to spend time with you.
You are interesting.
I love seeing the world your way.
It's good to be curious.

I love the way you tell stories.
What you did was awesome.
I admire you.
That's a great question.
Your friends are lucky to have you.
I trust you.
That was a really good choice.
Seeing you happy makes me happy.
Being your parent is my favorite job.
I learn new things from you every day.
You make me better.
You are a good boy/girl.
Thank you for being you.
I'm so glad you're here.
You look great.
I understand you.
Watching you grow up is the best.
That was really brave.
I forgive you.
I appreciate you.
We all make mistakes.
Yes, me too.
You are very good at that!
You can try again tomorrow.
Nobody is perfect.
I love how you said that.
Not everyone will like you, and that's OK.
You did that so well.
I'm listening.
That's a very fair point.
You are beautiful inside and out.

I love you.
I could never stop loving you.
You are enough.
You make my heart full.

Listening to help and make peace
How listening could change everything... March 21, 2018 Danielle Strickland
Peace making and LISTENING.

If there was ever a time for peace it's now. We need it. Badly. And I don't mean the kind of peace that keeps quiet. That's a kind of keeping the peace that disguises itself as nice and kind but is instead a deeply passive insistence on the status quo. People who 'keep the peace' have the luxury of willful blindness and are most likely those who have something to lose if true peace (justice/fairness/equality/rightness) was ever actually made. What we really need right now in our desperate world is true peace making. The kind Jesus suggested would usher in the Kingdom of God. Peace making - like trouble making but turned upside down.

Peacemaking - those with voices who stand out for the underdog and go out of their way to get in the way of injustice, exposing the deep and dark depths of racism, bigotry, abuse, and oppression in the desperate hope that exposure is the first stop on the train to healing. Peace creating is an active presence of goodwill in the world. It's a choice to pull our heads out of the sand and live into the realities of our contemporary global setting. There is so much peace to be created. But where to begin?

Recently, (AmplifyPeace.com) led a group of remarkable ladies on a peacemaking pilgrimage to the holy land. It was a vacation meant to diverge far from the ordinary one - going out of our way to get in the way of those who were suffering and prospering in the face of profound and horrific tyranny. We wanted to become involved in the reality of building peace, so we sought out individuals who were attempting to do exactly that. People trapped in the middle of the lengthy trauma of war but who were attempting to live a new life. People that looked and sounded a lot like Jesus.

We have a really basic structure that I believe would be beneficial to anybody who is asking how to become a peacemaker in their environment. Listen - Learn - Live.

The first means of building peace in the world is listening.

Listen. This is a lot tougher than it first sounds. Listening is an immensely essential technique for starting your peace-building quest. Listening is an act of solidarity with the person you are attempting to hear. And here is when we get a little specific. Whose voice have you not heard? And how can you begin to make some peace by choosing to listen to the voices of people whom you don't know? There is a great expression, 'an adversary is someone whose narrative you have not yet heard. At the center of every human being lies a sacred beginning. And to discover that the human heart may require some unearthing of our own bias and warped viewpoint and the only way to come to that heavenly connection of common humanity is to LISTEN to each other. Many of the individuals we assume we 'know about' we have not met. This is because the world is structured to keep us separate. To divide us. And this isolation develops anxiety and the fear keeps us in conflict. And tranquility is gone. So, peacemaking starts with deciding to walk in the opposite direction of tyranny and injustice. Connection. Those of us with the ability to select where we go and what we do and who we speak to may make the purposeful choice to LISTEN to those we have not yet heard.

In Israel that brought us to sit around tables and purposefully listen to Jews, Palestinians, Muslims, Christians, Atheists, Agnostics, women, men, boys, girls, teachers, moms, soldiers, rabbis, priests - well, you get the picture. To connect with many of those folks force us to travel to locations 'off the tourist map' and to position ourselves in some pain. It forced us to address our anxieties and prejudice and preconceived conceptions. But that is what listening needs us. Choice. We get to select who we listen to. But make no mistake, just because listening is basic doesn't make it easy. Active listening takes serious intention.

Chapter 5:**Know when your Kids need your attention something**

Parenting is considered one of the most difficult jobs in the world, but there's no formal education available on how to parent successfully. The good news is there are many ways parents can stimulate their babies' brains and use day-to-day events as exceptional learning opportunities.

Carlota Nelson, director of the documentary Brain Matters, outlines five straightforward, practical, and science-backed practices that can help set your baby up for future success.

1. Stimulate infant speaking and consider it as actual dialogue
The noises and actions that newborns produce may not always seem like much, but it's their sole means of communication. Early childhood development specialists think we should foster infant speaking and regard it as actual communication. Parents should listen to the baby's noises, signals, and movements and connect with them throughout the day. The quantity of words a newborn is exposed to will affect the number of words in

a child's vocabulary at age 2 and a child's reading levels later. Take infant babbling seriously and promote it.

2. Read to your infant to practice language
Babies may not be talking or reading yet but they're born ready to learn. Even at 3 months of age, kids can differentiate each sound used in every language on the whole planet. Every time you read out loud to your infant, you are establishing language abilities. Make careful to point to the photos in the book and ask questions about the plot and the characters. Simple queries like "what are they wearing?" and "how many are there?" can stimulate your child's linguistic skills. Reading to newborns not only introduces them to new words but also builds a passion for books and reading. Remember, leaders are readers, so why not start early?

3. Use ordinary occurrences as learning opportunities
For newborns, each life event is all about learning. Whether it's bath time, organizing clothes, cooking, or running errands, these activities are terrific learning opportunities. Narrate what you are doing to promote the language. Count and sort laundry to teach maths and play with food ingredients and textures to promote scientific thinking. Making faces that express various emotions is an excellent method to teach emotional intelligence.

4. Take play seriously
Young children are learning all the time. When they play, they're developing vital life skills. Make-believe play helps youngsters to experience what it's like to be someone else and comprehend others' sentiments. When they play with others, they're learning to negotiate and take turns. Engaging in creative free play, such as believing a toy train can go across space, promotes creativity and language as they begin to orally convey their thoughts. When they invent new worlds, young toddlers are learning to problem solve and create new possibilities. What seems like just fun is very important to work. Take play seriously because play is serious learning. Avoid being on your smartphone in front of your youngster too much. Research reveals that makes youngsters feel less significant.

5. Lead by example
Babies are brilliant impersonators. They take up on everything they watch you do. Until infants communicate, they become masters at reading faces and non-verbal attitudes and learn to emulate them. By seeing your body language, how you treat people or how you respond to a situation, infants will imitate these attitudes and behaviors themselves. The way you behave around your infant influences the person they will become.

Include these five critical behaviors in your day and you'll dramatically improve your baby's chances to thrive in the future. Giving your kid the finest skills for future success has nothing to do with money or costly learning supplies. It has everything to do with you, your time, and your degree of participation.

Summary \sEverything that modern parents need to know about caring for babies in the first 6 months, including step-by-step guidelines for getting babies on routine, hour-by-hour schedules at a glance, symptoms that warrant a trip to the emergency room, and feeding instructions for breast, bottle and both! But, the most common reason to read this book is to learn how to get your kid to sleep all night so you can too!

Many parents concentrate on their children's academics and extracurricular activities, such as making sure they study, finish their homework, and go to soccer practice or dancing classes on time. But all too often, we fail to spend time and effort cultivating another component of kid growth and development—one that is just as crucial, and probably even more essential—being a decent person.

It might be easy to ignore the necessity of fighting the overwhelming themes of rapid pleasure, materialism, and selfishness present in our culture.

If we want to raise children who are truly lovely individuals, we may assist steer our kids toward habits and behaviors that encourage desirable character qualities like kindness, generosity, and empathy for others who are less advantaged or who need aid.

As C.S. Lewis famously remarked, "Integrity is doing the right thing, even when no one is watching." How do we raise a decent kid, one who will do the right thing, even when no one may see them do it, and when there may be no reward? While there is no definite recipe (if only!), here are some ways parents may cultivate strong character and help their kids grow into decent people.

Nurture Empathy in Your Child
Emotional intelligence and empathy, or the capacity to put oneself in someone else's shoes and consider their emotions and ideas, is one of the most important attributes in excellent individuals. Studies have indicated that having a high emotional quotient—that is, being able to comprehend one's own emotions and the feelings of others—Is a significant component of success in life. 1

To foster empathy in your kid, encourage your child to communicate about her emotions and make sure she understands that you care about them. When a quarrel develops with a friend, advise her to consider how her buddy could be feeling and offer her techniques of regulating her emotions and work productively toward a settlement.

Encourage Them to Lift Others

While tales of kids participating in bullying and other negative conduct frequently make headlines, the fact is that many youngsters quietly accomplish good things in the usual course of their lives, whether it's helping a buddy feel better when he's down or pitching in at a community center.

As you encourage positive behaviors such as doing something to make someone's day better (even something as small as patting a friend on the shoulder when they're sad), be sure to talk about what negative effects behaviors like gossiping or bullying have on both sides (both those who are bullied and those who do the bullying), and why and how it hurts people.

Teach Them to Volunteer

Whether your child helps an elderly neighbor by shoveling the sidewalk or helps you pack some canned goods into boxes for donation to family shelters, the act of volunteering can shape your child's character. When kids serve others, they learn to think about the needs of people less fortunate than they are, and may feel proud of themselves for making a difference in others' lives.

Offer Rewards Sparingly

An essential thing to remember when teaching youngsters to assist others is to not praise them for every single nice act. That way, your youngster won't equate volunteering with earning stuff for himself and will learn that feeling good about helping others will be in itself a reward.

That's not to say you shouldn't occasionally take your child out for a special treat or give them a gift for helping others AND for working hard and studying hard.

Kids love encouragement and thrive on parents' approval. An occasional reward is a great way to show him how thankful you are for the good things he does.

Teach Them Good Manners
Does your youngster consistently practice the foundations of good manners such as saying "Thank you" and "Please"? Does she talk in a respectful way to others and address seniors as "Mr." and Ms."? Does she know how to greet people properly, and is she familiar with the basics of good table manners? Is she a gracious loser when she plays a game with friends?

Remember that you are raising a child who will go out into the world and interact with people for the rest of her life. (And this small person, as she develops, will be at the dinner table with you and engaging with you every day until she leaves the nest.) You can play an important role in shaping how well-mannered your child will be.

Treat Them With Kindness and Respect

The most effective way to get kids to speak to you and others respectfully and to interact with others sufficiently is by doing exactly that yourself when you interact with your child. Think about how you talk to your kid.

Do you speak harshly when you're not happy about something? Do you ever rant or say things that are not nice? Consider your style of speaking, behaving, and even thinking, and try to use a kind and courteous tone and attitude with your kid, even when you are talking to him about a mistake or disobedience.

Discipline Your Child Consistently
Parents who hold back on giving children limits or strongly (but compassionately) addressing poor conduct may potentially be damaging their kids with good intentions. Children who are not disciplined are rude, selfish, and shockingly sad.

Some of the numerous reasons why we need discipline include the fact that children who are given clear rules, limits, and expectations are responsible, more self-sufficient, more likely to make good choices, and more likely to make friends and be happy. As soon as you observe behavior issues like lying or backtalk, treat them with compassion, understanding, and firmness.

5 Discipline Strategies That Work
Teach Them to Be Thankful
Teaching your kid how to be thankful and how to show that appreciation is a critical component of raising a

healthy child. Whether it's for a dish you've made for supper or a birthday present from Grandma and Grandpa, educate your youngster to say thank you. For things like gifts for birthdays and holidays, be sure your child gets into the habit of writing thank you cards.

Give Them Responsibilities

When children have an anticipated list of age-appropriate jobs to undertake at home, such as helping prepare the table or cleaning the floor, they build a feeling of responsibility and success. Doing a good job and feeling like they are contributing to the welfare of the home may make youngsters feel proud of themselves, and help them become happy.

Why You Should Be Giving Your Kids More Chores\sModel Good Behavior

Consider how you interact with others, even when your child isn't watching. Do you say "Thank you" to the checkout clerk at the market? Do you keep clear of chatter regarding neighbors or co-workers? Do you employ a nice tone while approaching waiters? You directly influence how your children will be. If you want to raise a decent kid, behave yourself in the manner you want your child to act.

Chapter 6:**DISCIPLINE**

8 Ways to Discipline Your Child Without Spanking
By Amy Morin, LCSW Updated on September 17, 2020
Medically reviewed by Ann-Louise T. Lockhart, PsyD, ABPP

Spanking is one of the most hotly contested parenting subjects. While most pediatricians and parenting experts don't recommend spanking,1 the vast majority of parents around the world admit to spanking their kids.

For many parents, spanking can feel like the fastest and most effective way to change a child's behavior. And it often works in the short term. But, research reveals physical punishment has long-term implications for youngsters.

If you're searching for an alternative to spanking, here are eight techniques to discipline your kid without using physical punishment.

1\sTime-Out
There are numerous methods to discipline kids without hitting them.
Comstock/Stockbyte/Getty Images
Hitting kids for misbehavior (especially aggression) sends a mixed message. Your kid will question why it's OK for you to strike them, but not OK for them to hit their sibling. Placing a youngster in time-out might be a far better solution. 1 When done appropriately, time-out

teaches youngsters how to calm themselves down, which is an important life skill.

But for a time-out to be successful, kids need to have lots of pleasant time-in with their parents. Then, when they're removed from a situation, they will begin to learn to self-regulate, appropriately express their emotions, and make different choices in the future.

2\sLosing Privileges
The idea is not to punish your kid into submission, but to help them learn to make better choices for the future. This takes practice, though. If they make a bad decision, educate them that the penalty is a loss of a privilege. The loss should be related to the behavior.

Make it clear when the privileges may be gained back. Usually, 24 hours is long enough to educate your youngster to learn from their error. So you may say, "You've lost TV for the rest of the day, but you can earn it back tomorrow by tidying up your toys the first time I ask."

3\sIgnoring Mild Misbehavior
Selective ignoring may be more effective than spanking.
1
This doesn't imply you should look the other way if your kid is doing anything harmful or improper. But you can disregard attention-seeking conduct.

When your kid attempts to obtain attention by whining or moaning, don't give it to them. Look the other way, like you can't hear them and don't answer. Then, when they ask sweetly or behave, return your focus to them. Over time, they will learn that polite behavior is the best way to get their needs met.

4\sTeaching New Skills
One of the main problems with spanking is that it doesn't teach your child how to behave better. Spanking your child because they threw a temper tantrum won't teach them how to calm down the next time they are upset.

Kids benefit from learning how to problem-solve, manage their emotions, and compromise. When parents teach these skills, it can greatly reduce behavior problems. Use discipline that is intended at educating, not punishing.

5\sLogical Consequences
Logical consequences are a terrific technique to assist youngsters who are suffering from particular behavior issues. Logical repercussions are explicitly related to the wrongdoing.

For example, if your child doesn't eat their dinner, don't let them have a bedtime snack. Or if they refuse to pick up their trucks, don't allow them to play with them for the rest of the day. Linking the punishment directly to the behavior issue helps youngsters learn that their choices have clear repercussions.

6\sNatural Consequences
Natural consequences enable youngsters to learn from their errors. For example, if your kid declares they are not going to wear a jacket, let them walk outdoors and be cold—as long as it's safe to do so. Use natural consequences when you believe your kid will learn from their own mistake. Monitor the situation to ensure that your child won't experience any real danger.

7\sRewards for Good Behavior
Instead of punishing a youngster for disobedience, praise them for good conduct. For example, if your kid argues with their siblings regularly, put up an incentive system to urge them to get along better.

Providing an incentive to behave may turn around misbehavior swiftly. Rewards assist youngsters to concentrate on what they need to accomplish to obtain privileges, rather than stress the negative conduct they're expected to avoid.

8\sPraise for Good Behavior
Prevent behavior issues by capturing your youngster behaving well.
1
For example, when they are playing nicely with their siblings, point it out. Say, "You are doing such a terrific job sharing and taking turns today."

When there are several children in the room, give the most attention and praise to the children who are following the rules and behaving well. Then, when the other kid starts to behave, offer them praise and attention as well.

Parenting may be plain stressful and unpleasant. Your kids have a lot of needs that need to be met and even more wishes and want they'd like you to take care of. Before you melt down under the stress of parenting consider this simple advice; take care of yourself so you can take care of your family.

Parents and caregivers who pay attention to their mental, emotional and physical health are better able to handle the challenges that come with raising kids. Studies show those parents and caregivers adapt to changes, recover from setbacks, and build stronger relationships. Studies have demonstrated that parents and caregivers of children with developmental and mental health concerns are considerably more likely to suffer; sadness, anxiety, marital troubles, exhaustion, and sleeplessness.

Any amount of time you can take for yourself is incredibly vital. Even five minutes a day might be a powerful reminder of who you are in a bigger sense. It may assist protect you from being absorbed by your daily or hourly tasks.

Here are some tips to practice healthy mental habits;

Notice the positive: When you take the time to notice positive moments in your day, your experience of that day becomes better. Write down one item each day or week that was wonderful, even if the positive thing appears little it's real and it matters and may start to transform how you see and experience life.

Avoid the feeling of guilt: When you allow yourself to notice your feelings without judging them as good or bad, you dial down the stress and feel more in control. When you feel less stressed, you're better able to thoughtfully choose how to act.

Set time aside for you and your spouse: Prioritize date evenings! As parents, it can be easy to forget that your relationship needs some attention too! Get a babysitter or call on the help of a friend or family member to watch the kids. Prioritize date nights or outings where it's just you and your spouse or partner. It can also help to remind you why you're together in the first place.

Revisit activities you like doing: Revisit the things you enjoyed before driving to soccer practice took over your life or acquire a new passion. You need an outlet to reset and reflect without the constant needs of your kids taking priority.

Accept there are limitations to what you can do: The idea that you are the only one who can help or care for a child or loved one will cause burnout. Don't be afraid to ask for help.

Avoid the feeling of isolation: Find a support network outside of your immediate family or spend time with friends who have no connection to your child.

You may feel that you don't have time to socialize with friends or build new friendships. Try to concentrate on the long term. If you can meet up with a friend once a month or go to a community event or something similar once every two months, it still helps keeps you connected. Being a parent is an amazing and important part of your life, but it's not the entire story. Please keep in mind, some parents may need to consult a doctor or family physician to manage severe stress or to diagnose a more serious issue that needs medical attention.

Allow your child to copy you in good behavior

raise brilliant kids

The pride of any parent is to raise kids with adaptable, resilient, and clever minds. Kids who perform below such expectations are frequently a cause of stress to their parents.

However, according to a neuroscientist-cum-psychologist at the Harvard Medical School and Massachusetts General Hospital in the United States, Lisa Barrett, how intellectual a child is primarily relying on the parents and not the kid per se.

"A child's brain is not a small adult brain. It is a brain born under construction that links itself to the world. And it's up to parents to create a world – both physical and social – that is rich with wiring instructions," Barrett writes on cnbc.com.

The psychologist and others provide the following parenting rules to raise smart children. The experts note that the tips are based on years of research in neuroscience and psychology.

Be a gardener, not a carpenter

Barrett recommends adopting the "gardener approach" rather than the "carpenter approach" when raising children.

She says, "Carpenters carve wood into the shape they want. Gardeners assist things to develop on their own by nurturing a fertile setting. Likewise, parents may mold their kid into something special, like, a concert violinist. Or they can provide an environment that encourages healthy growth in whatever direction the child takes.

"You might want your kid to play the violin in Symphony Hall someday, but forcing them to take lessons (the carpenter approach) might build a virtuoso or a kid who views music as an unpleasant chore.

"The gardener approach would be to sprinkle a variety of musical opportunities around the home and see which ones spark your child's interest. Do they love to bang on pots and pans? Maybe your child is a budding heavy metal drummer."

Barrett adds that "once you understand what kind of 'plant' you're growing, you can 'adjust the soil' for it to take root and flourish."

Talk and read to your child a lot

According to Barrett, research shows that even when children are just a few months old and don't understand the meanings of words, their brains still make use of them.

The scientist explains that this develops a brain foundation for eventual learning and that the more words they hear, the stronger the impact. She says that students will also have greater vocabulary and reading comprehension.

She continues, "Teaching kids 'emotion words' (i.e., sad, pleased, annoyed) is extremely useful. The more they know, the more flexibly they can act.

"Put this advice into action by elaborating on the feelings of other people. Talk about what generates emotions and how they could impact someone: 'See that weeping boy? He is feeling pain from falling and scraping his knee. He is sad and probably wants a hug from his parents.'

"Think of yourself as your children's tour guide through the mysterious world of humans and their movements and sounds."

Explain things to them

Although it can be exhausting when your child is constantly asking, "Why?" But when you explain something to them, you've taken something new and novel from the world and made it predictable.

Barrett says to avoid answering "why" questions with, "Because I said so" – noting that children who understand the reasons to behave in a particular way can more effectively regulate their actions.

She explains, "If all kids know is, 'I shouldn't eat all the cookies because an authority person told me so, and I'll get in trouble,' that logic may not assist when parents aren't around.

"It's better if youngsters realize, 'I shouldn't eat all the cookies because I'll have a stomachache, and my brother and sister will be sad at missing dessert.' This thinking helps kids grasp the repercussions of their actions and promotes empathy."

Help your children to imitate you

Have you noticed how certain things that look like labor to you (i.e., cleaning the home or weeding a garden) may be a play to a child? Barrett observes that youngsters learn naturally by observing, playing, and most of all, by emulating adults.

"It's an efficient method to learn, and it offers them a feeling of mastery. So throw them a little broom or garden shovel or a toy lawnmower and let the imitation begin," she advises.

Likewise, a US-based psychologist and writer Jenny Marchal, adds that when parents do clever things, their children will likewise do intelligent things.

"Kids pick up on all kinds of things, notably your acts. Learning by adult conduct is one of the key ways a youngster takes up habits and makes sense of the environment. If your kid sees you involved in reading, writing, or anything creative, it will inspire them to copy you and get smarter in the process," Marchal says on lifehack.org.

Don't overprotect them

In today's world of fast-paced parenting, US-based child development specialist Eric Dodge decries that many parents have difficulties letting their kids solve issues, but rather hurry to address obstacles for them.

Also, based on Harvard University research, a child specialist and author Julie Lythcott-Haims says that enabling kids to make errors and build resilience and resourcefulness is crucial in setting them up for success. **"This isn't easy. We all need to walk a fine line between protecting our children and letting them tackle problems in order to learn from them," she writes on time.com.**

Similarly, Marchal says allowing one's child to take risks and failing will teach them fundamental life skills from an early age.

She says, "Without experiencing failure early on, a child can develop low self-esteem and get discouraged from creating and learning for themselves. Fear is probably the number one emotion in our lives that can stop us from taking

great actions. If we encourage our children to experience failure when they are small, the amount of fear they develop will lessen.

Related News
"Teaching a child that failure is not actually a bad thing is a great life skill that will allow them to make smart decisions and learn from life's ups and downs. At the end of the day, children need to feel emotions to understand them and protecting your child from them will only stunt their ability to adapt and make sense of the world."

Regulate their screen time

According to Lythcott-Haims, too much screen time has been linked to childhood obesity, irregular sleep patterns, and behavioural issues.

In addition, a 2017 study by researchers at the University of Montreal in Canada revealed that playing "shooter" games can damage the brain, causing it to lose cells.

So what can we do about the ever-so-helpful digital babysitter that so many of us rely on?

The American Academy of Paediatrics recommends keeping entertainment "screen time" to a maximum of two hours per day.

"Another useful suggestion is to encourage your kids to create content rather than just consume it. Turn screen time into a productive activity by encouraging them to learn computer programming, 3D modeling, or digital music production, advises Lythcott-Haims.

Dodge also suggests teaching kids social skills to replace screen time.

He cites a 20-year study conducted by Duke and Pennsylvania State University researchers that demonstrates a link between kindergarten social skills and early adult success.

It's a good idea to begin by teaching your children how to solve problems with their friends, share their possessions, listen without interrupting, and assist family members, suggests Dodge.

Spend fewer words praising their appearance.

Experts advise against praising children too much for their innate abilities, such as intelligence or beauty. These unsatisfying comments include: "Wow, you got an A without even studying? You are so wise.

According to a Stanford University research, complimenting kids' intelligence with words like the one above can actually cause them to perform below expectations.

Parents are urged to utilize praise that emphasizes the effort children make to overcome obstacles by exhibiting grit, tenacity, and determination as an alternative parenting method.

Aim for a caring and calm household

Children in high-conflict homes typically do worse than children of parents who get along, according to a number of studies. Therefore, raising healthy and successful children requires providing a caring, supporting atmosphere.

Mrs. Funmi Oladeji, a counselor in Lagos, tells Saturday PUNCH that it's crucial for parents to avoid fighting, especially in front of their kids. But if it does, the parents should deal with it in front of their kids. The children are left with the sense that their parents always work things out, even when there is a misunderstanding.

"Therefore, they are inclined to apologize if they insult someone else too. In a family where a kid is being nurtured, harmony and resolve are crucial qualities to have.

Avoid being too stiff or overly soft.

Diana Baumrind divided between authoritarian (very harsh), permissive (extremely lenient), and authoritative (equally disciplined and caring) parents in her ground-breaking 1966 study.

In summary, permissive parents are too soft, authoritarian parents are exactly right, and authoritative parents are in the middle.

According to Dodge's article on Inc.com, children develop the social awareness and emotion management abilities that are essential for success by imitating their authoritarian parents.

Children should be exposed to many individuals (safely).

Try to expose your children to as much diversity as you can, especially when they are young, along with others they may typically encounter, such as grandparents, aunts, uncles, acquaintances, and other children.

According to studies, young children who routinely interact with people who speak other languages may keep vital brain connections that may aid their future language learning.

Similar to adults, infants who view a wide array of faces may develop neural pathways that help them recognize and recall a wider range of faces in the future. The simplest anti-racism action you can take as a parent may be this, Barrett says.

In the meanwhile, Dodge suggests giving youngsters work since it will make them more intelligent.

According to him, there is a lot of evidence that chores are good for children's growth. However, just 28% of parents in a Braun Research survey indicated they often give their kids work. According to data analysis conducted by the University of Minnesota, whether or not young children had duties when they were three or four years old was the best indicator of success as an adult.

Always monitor your kids' conduct
Child behavior red flags
Hugo Lin's illustration for Verywell, 2018.
Sometimes regulations should be broken by kids. They discover things about themselves and the world by pushing their limitations. They learn valuable lessons through the repercussions you impose on them.

However, in certain cases, behavioral issues may be an indication of a more serious condition. It's critical to have some understanding of child development in order to distinguish between typical and atypical behavior problems. For a teenager, what is typical for a preschooler is not typical for them.

Normal Preschool Conduct
It's common for preschoolers to debate and exercise their freedom to say "no" as they strive for independence. They frequently oscillate between insisting they are an independent big kid who can handle everything and using baby speak to beg for assistance with a basic activity.

While preschoolers may have the occasional temper tantrum, they should be doing better at managing their emotions and impulses than they were as toddlers. At this age, temper outbursts should be milder than during the toddler years.

Children between the ages of 4 and 5 may occasionally act aggressively, but they should be taught to resolve conflicts via dialogue rather than physical force.

1

Normal Behaviour in Children of School Age
Children in elementary school frequently demand more independence than they can handle as they take on more responsibilities. When it comes to doing chores, doing their schoolwork, and taking care of their hygiene, they probably need a considerable lot of coaching. As they start to take

on more responsibility and try out new things, they could find it difficult to accept failure.

It's typical for grade schoolers to require some assistance in managing unpleasant emotions, such as impatience and worry, and it's also typical for them to lack verbal impulse control.

Normal Tween Behavior
When children reach their adolescent years, their attitude toward their parents generally reflects their burgeoning independence. As they start to want to distance themselves from their parents, it's typical for tweens to be moderately defiant and argumentative. 3

Tweens may have trouble making friends and may experience frequent arguments with them. Additionally, they frequently lack the capacity to comprehend how their actions may affect them in the long run. Tweens want uplifting reinforcement for their good behavior throughout these challenging adolescent years.

Give special attention to teaching your child social and life skills, such as how to shake someone's hand or wash the dishes. Take advantage of instructional moments and help your child learn from their errors.

Teens' Typical Behavior
Teenagers may believe themselves to be grownups, yet they still want assistance in making wise choices. As your kid works to define who they are as a person, be ready to cope with a number of phases they may go through. Teenagers frequently experiment with different haircuts, clothing, and social groupings as they strive to define their identities.

When it comes to finishing their tasks or their assignments on time, teenagers should have more self-discipline. They might still be rather cranky, and a little disobedience and moderate non-compliance are OK.

Teenagers frequently wish to prove to their parents that they are capable of making their own decisions, thus little rebellion is typical.

3

It's crucial to create clear standards and stick to them as long as your teen is in your home.

Worry Time
When compared to what is developmentally acceptable, these broad warning indicators could point to more severe behavioral issues. Speak to your child's doctor if you have worries about their conduct. They can assist you in deciding if your

child's conduct is typical or whether a professional referral is necessary.

Problems Managing Emotions

While occasional tantrums in toddlers are common, older kids should be able to deal with their emotions in a way that is acceptable to their peers. Your kid may have an underlying emotional issue if they are unable to manage their frustration, rage, or disappointment in a way that is age-appropriate.

erratic impulse control

Over time, impulse control gradually improves. Children who become combative after starting school or kids who shout at their teachers as teenagers probably require assistance in improving their abilities.

Failure to React to Punishment

Children occasionally repeat their errors to test if their parents will enforce consequences. However, if you're using consistent discipline, it's not typical for a youngster to display the same conduct over. It may be an issue like oppositional defiance disorder if your child persists in misbehaving regardless of the repercussions.

Challenges at School

It is not appropriate to disregard behavior that disrupts school. A learning deficiency or underlying behavior condition may be indicated by this behaviour. Potential red flags include being dismissed from class, getting into conflicts at recess, and having trouble focusing.

Problems Interacting Socially

Concern arises when a person's conduct obstructs social engagement. Kids fight with their classmates sometimes, but if your child's conduct makes it difficult for them to make friends, that's a problem. It is important for kids to be able to form and maintain positive relationships with their peers.

Sexualized Conduct

Undevelopmentally appropriate sexualized activities are a red flag, frequently indicating exposure to trauma or sexual abuse. It's common for youngsters to be interested in the other sex and wonder where infants come from. However, coerced sexual activity is never acceptable, regardless of age.

Self-Injury

You should take notice if somebody (adult or child) injures themselves. A mental health specialist should assess a person's conduct if they bang their head, burn themselves, or cut themselves. 4 A youngster should be assessed by a professional if there is any discussion of suicide.

Call the National Suicide Prevention Lifeline at 988 for support and guidance from a qualified counselor if your kid is contemplating suicide. Call 911 if you or a loved one is in urgent danger.

Visit our National Helpline Database for additional information on mental health resources.

Message From Verywell
You may frequently solve minor behavioral issues by altering your approach to discipline. Look for strategies to improve the effectiveness of discipline. Consider using a positive penalty that encourages your child to complete their schoolwork instead of, say, grounding them. Professional assistance is necessary for more severe behavioral issues. A school counselor or your family physician can recommend someone.

What Kind of Punishment Works Best for My Child?
mother-daughter guidance
Teaching your child to behave is one of your responsibilities as a parent. It's a task that requires both patience and time. But learning efficient and beneficial methods of discipline is beneficial.

The American Academy of Pediatrics (AAP) has provided some advice on how to help your child learn appropriate behavior as they get older.

10 productive healthy discipline techniques

The AAP advises using positive discipline techniques to train kids to control their behavior, protect them from harm, and foster healthy development. These consist of:

"Show and tell" Children can learn well from wrong through calm words and deeds. Show your kids how to behave by setting an example.

Set boundaries. Make sure your children can obey your clear and consistent guidelines. Make careful to convey these guidelines in language that is suitable for their age.

impose penalties. Explain the repercussions if kids don't behave in a forceful yet calm manner. Tell her, for instance, that you will put her toys away for the rest of the day if she doesn't tidy them up. Be prepared to act immediately after. Don't give in by returning them after a short while. Never deprive your child of anything they need, like a meal.

Let them speak. It is crucial to listen. Before assisting with the solution, let your youngster finish the narrative. Watch for instances when bad conduct tends to repeat itself, such as when your youngster is feeling envious. Instead of merely imposing punishment, have a conversation with your youngster about this.

Pay attention to them. Attention is the most effective weapon for punishment since it can both deter bad conduct and reinforce good behavior. Keep in mind that all kids desire their parents' attention.

Observe them doing well. Children should be taught to recognize both excellent and poor behavior. Observe positive conduct and call it out, rewarding accomplishments and sincere efforts. Give examples, such as "Wow, you did a terrific job putting that toy away!"

Know when to avoid responding. Ignoring poor behavior can be an excellent method to end it, provided your child isn't engaging in anything risky and receives lots of praise for good conduct. Children can learn about the repercussions of their actions by being taught to ignore poor conduct. For instance, if your toddler intentionally drops her cookies, she will quickly run out of cookies to eat. She won't be allowed to play with her toy if she tosses it and breaks it. It won't take her long to figure out how to play with her toys responsibly and stop dropping her cookies.

Be ready for difficulty. Prepare in advance for scenarios in which your kid may struggle with behavior. Get them ready for forthcoming events and the behavior you desire from them.

redirect undesirable behavior. Children may misbehave occasionally if they are bored or ignorant of better behavior. Find your youngster something else to do.

Time out is needed. A time-out is particularly helpful when a particular rule is breached. Children are best warned that they will have a time out if they don't stop acting out, reminded of their wrongdoing in the fewest possible words and without showing any emotion, and then removed from the environment for a predetermined amount of time (1 minute per year of age is a good rule of thumb). You can try letting your kids lead their time-out instead of setting a timer with kids who are at least 3 years old. You can just say, "Go to time out and come back when you feel ready and in control." This technique, which can aid in the child's learning and practice of self-management abilities, is equally effective with older kids and teenagers.

Harsh language and spanking are destructive and ineffective. This is why:
The AAP's "Effective Discipline to Raise Healthy Children" policy statement outlines the benefits of emphasizing teaching appropriate conduct above punishing inappropriate behavior. According to research, spanking, slapping, and other physical punishments are ineffective at changing a child's conduct. The same is true if you scold or shout at a

youngster. Harsh physical and verbal punishments can harm a child's long-term physical and mental health in addition to being ineffectual.

The harmful cycle of spanking. Parents and other adults who care for children are advised not to strike or spank them by the AAP. Spanking frequently makes kids more aggressive and angry and intolerant of others instead of teaching responsibility and self-control. In a study of children born in 20 major U.S. cities, it was shown that families who spanked their kids became stuck in a vicious cycle: the more spankings they received, the more they misbehaved later on, which led to more spankings. The repercussions of spanking can extend beyond the parent-child bond. Because it teaches that hurting someone when you're angry is acceptable—even with somebody you love. When they don't receive what they want, children who are spanked may be more prone to hit other people.

permanent traces. Physical punishment may have additional observable effects on the brain and body and raises the chance of damage, particularly in infants under the age of 18 months. Spanking causes children to have greater amounts of hormones linked to toxic stress. Physical punishment could also have an impact on brain growth. According to one research, children who received frequent spankings had less gray matter, the area of the brain responsible for self-control, and they did worse on IQ tests as children than the control group.

Words that hurt: verbal abuse. It has been shown that yelling at children and using words to inflict emotional suffering or disgrace is ineffectual and detrimental. Even by parents who are usually warm and caring, harsh verbal discipline can cause greater disobedience and mental health issues in kids. According to research, adolescents' behavior issues and signs of melancholy may increase as a result of the harsh verbal discipline that is increasingly widespread as kids become older.
Learn from your errors as well.
Keep in mind that if you feel out of control as a parent, you may take time out for yourself. Just make sure your child is secure before giving yourself some time to breathe deeply, unwind, or phone a friend. Go back to your child, cuddle them, and restart when you are feeling better.

Try not to worry if you don't manage a problem well the first time. Consider what you could have done better and make an effort to implement it the next time. If you believe you made a serious error in judgment in the heat of the moment, wait until you have calmed down before you apologize to your child and explain how you plan to handle the matter going forward. Make careful you honor your commitment. This serves as a fantastic example for your youngster of how to learn from errors.

Guidelines for healthy & productive discipline by age/stage

Infants Babies observe what you do, so set examples of the behavior you want to see.

To help your infant learn, talk pleasantly. Say "Time to sit," as opposed to "Don't stand," as an example.

Reserving the word "no" for the most crucial matters, like safety, makes sense. Limit the necessity of saying "no" by keeping harmful or alluring items out of reach.

At this age, it is wise to divert attention and swap out a harmful or banned toy for one that is OK to play with.

Talk with your spouse, family, and child care provider to establish some ground rules that everyone will abide by since all children, even infants, require regular discipline.

Toddlers

Your child is beginning to understand what is acceptable and what is not, but they may test some of the rules to see how you respond. Pay attention to the behaviors you wish to encourage, and highlight them, while ignoring the opposite. When necessary, switch to a new activity.

As your child strives to adapt to new settings and skills, tantrums may become more frequent. Be aware of potential tantrum triggers, like hunger or exhaustion, and assist prevent them by timing naps and meals.

Teach your child to avoid hitting, biting, or engaging in other aggressive actions. Avoid smacking your child and resolve disagreements with your partner amicably to set a good example for others.

Maintain consistency in setting boundaries. If necessary, try using brief timeouts.

Recognize sibling rivalries but refrain from taking sides. For instance, if a dispute erupts over a toy, the object might be stored away.

Age of Preschoolers Children in the preschool years are still learning how and why things happen as well as the effects of their activities. Expect children to keep pushing the boundaries set by their parents and siblings as they learn proper conduct.

Start giving them age-appropriate tasks, like putting their toys away. Give straightforward, detailed instructions. Praise them as a reward.

While redirecting and establishing reasonable boundaries, let your youngster choose among appropriate options.

Teach your kid to treat people the way you would like to be treated.

Explain that while occasionally feeling angry is OK, hurting someone or breaking items is not. Teach them constructive strategies for handling anger, such as talking about it.

Use time-outs or get rid of the source of the issue to settle disputes.

Children at Grade School
Your youngster is starting to understand what is morally right and wrong. Discuss the alternatives available to them in trying circumstances, the advantages and disadvantages of each, and the outcomes of their actions.

Discuss family expectations and appropriate punishments for disobeying them.

Give youngsters a healthy mix of advantages and responsibilities, increasing their privileges as long as they behave well.

Maintain your efforts to impart and exemplify tolerance, care, and respect for others.

Don't allow yourself or others to punish you physically. You have the right to prohibit spanking your child if you reside in a region where it is permitted in schools.

Teens & Adolescents
You must strike a balance between your unwavering love and support for your kid and the establishment of clear expectations, guidelines, and boundaries.

Continue to provide her with a lot of love and attention. Talk to someone every day. If young people maintain relationships with their families, they are more likely to make good decisions.

Learn about your teen's peers and have a courteous and responsible connection discussion.